INSECT WATCHING

Written by Ruth Thomson and Margaret Stephens
Series Editor Sue Jacquemier
Consultant Editor Anthony Wootton
Editorial revision by Margaret Stephens
Designed by Nick Eddison and Sally Burrough
Design revision by Julia Rheam

Illustrated by John Barber, Stephen Bennett,
Roland Berry, Lynn Chadwick, Don Forrest, Chris
Howell-Jones, Ian Jackson, Roger Kent, Colin King, Richard
Lewington, Josephine Martin, Doreen McGuinness, Charles
Raymond, Phillip Richardson, Jim Robins, David Watson,
Phil Weare, Adrian Williams, Roy Wiltshire

Bumble bee

Forester moth

Chalk hill blue butterfly

Insects are almost everywhere. You will find them in the garden, under the bark of trees, on walls and inside your home. This book tells you all about common European insects. You will discover how tiny caterpillars turn into adult butterflies, which insects live around ponds, and how grasshoppers sing. This book also shows you how to keep insects and make notes about them.

Wherever possible, the insects have been drawn life size. Where lengths are given, they refer to the length of the insect from the tip of its abdomen to its head, not including the antennae. When the wing span is given, this is a measurement from wing-tip to wing-tip.

In the other *NatureTrail* books the species names of animals and birds have capital letters. But many insects are commonly known by their family names, which do not have capital letters. Therefore, insect names in this book are written without capital letters.

Seven-spot ladybird

Common blue butterfly

Peacock butterfly

INSECT WATCHING

Contents

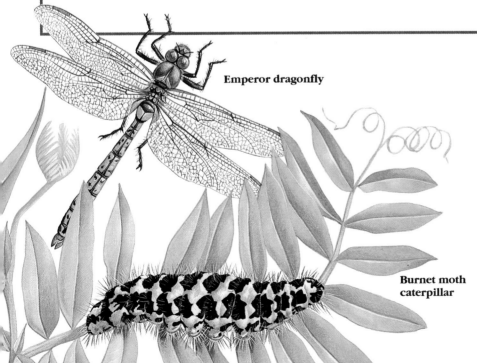

Emperor dragonfly

Burnet moth
caterpillar

This edition published in 1993
First published in 1976 by
Usborne Publishing Ltd
Usborne House
83-85 Saffron Hill
London EC1N 8RT
England

Text and Artwork © 1993, 1985, 1976
by Usborne Publishing Ltd.

The name Usborne and the device are
Trade Marks of Usborne Publishing Ltd.

Printed in Belgium.

Becoming an insect watcher

It is easy to become an insect watcher because it is never difficult to find insects. You can spot them in most places. Look first at as many types as you can, to learn how they are different from other animals. Later you may want to study one or two types in more detail.

There are more different types of insects (called species) than all the different kinds of mammals, fish, birds and reptiles put together. People are still discovering many new species and finding out more about those already known.

What is an insect?

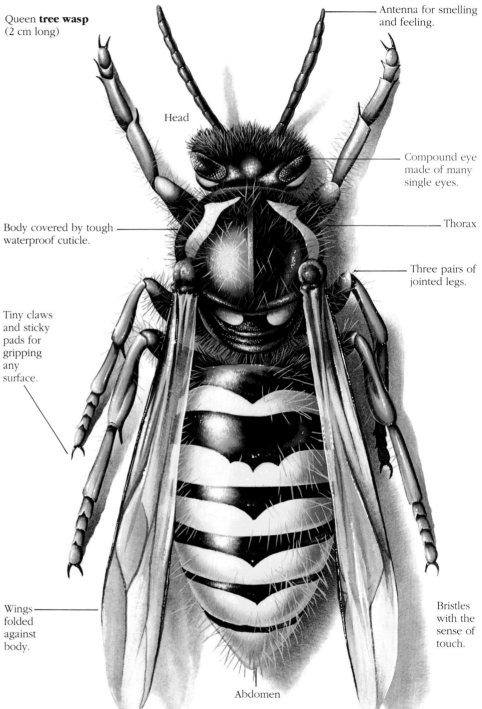

Queen **tree wasp** (2 cm long)

Antenna for smelling and feeling.

Head

Compound eye made of many single eyes.

Body covered by tough waterproof cuticle.

Thorax

Three pairs of jointed legs.

Tiny claws and sticky pads for gripping any surface.

Wings folded against body.

Bristles with the sense of touch.

Abdomen

These are not insects

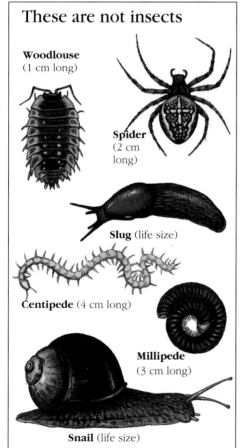

Woodlouse (1 cm long)

Spider (2 cm long)

Slug (life size)

Centipede (4 cm long)

Millipede (3 cm long)

Snail (life size)

Only insects have three body parts and three pairs of legs. Slugs and snails have no legs. Spiders have eight legs. The bodies of millipedes, centipedes and woodlice have lots of parts, called segments. Most of these segments have legs on them.

All adult insects have three parts to their bodies. These are: a head, a thorax (middle) and an abdomen (lower part). On their heads they have a pair of antennae, used mainly for smelling and feeling. Most insects have a pair of large eyes made up of many tiny eyes. At some time in their lives all insects will have three pairs of jointed legs attached to the thorax. Some insect legs may have a special job to do. For example, they may have a tiny pocket for collecting pollen. Others may be flat with hairs to help the insect swim. Apart from birds and bats, insects are the only other kind of animal that can fly properly.

What you need

These are some of the things it is useful to have if you want to be an insect watcher. You will need a good pocket lens and a field notebook for recording what you see. Choose a lens which magnifies 8 or 10 times. It is a good idea to fix it on some string round your neck, to keep it handy. You may not need all the things shown. This will depend on where you want to look for insects.

If you have a pocket-size book on insects, carry it with you and indentify the insects as you spot them.

Spiral-bound notebook (see right).

A butterfly net may be useful. Stalk the insect slowly and quietly. Do not harm it and do not keep it captive for long.

Lay a white sheet under a bush. Gently knock the bush with a stick. The sheet will catch falling insects.

Trowel

A small trowel is useful for digging up earth. Sieve the soil to find insects.

Mark an area with string (about 1 m square). Count the insects you find there. Now count insects in another area the same size. Compare the results.

Take a bag with pockets to carry your equipment in.

Carry insects in screw-top jars or boxes lined with paper or moss.

Keeping a notebook

It is best to use a spiral-bound notebook for your notes. Then you can tear off pages and keep together all the notes you have made at different times on a particular insect. Make rough notes when you are actually watching the insect. Make more careful ones later. Write down the date and the time when you saw the insect and what the weather was like. Try to describe the insect and the plant you found it on as fully as possible. If you want to return to an insect, draw a map to guide you.

Quick sketches

Make quick sketches of the insects you find. When you get home, look them up and try to identify them.

Head   Thorax   Abdomen

Draw three ovals for the head, thorax and abdomen.

Draw the insect's legs and antennae in position.

Draw in the wings, if the insect has any.

Add any special markings or colours if you have time.

Differences to spot

It is not always easy to tell one insect from another. Some flies look very like bees, while many bugs look like beetles. There are lots of different species of insect - many more than a million in the world.

When you are taking notes on an insect you have found, try to make a habit of asking yourself several questions. Does it have wings? How many pairs of wings? Does the insect have hard wing-cases? The charts on these pages show some of the insects which have these features.

This is not a scientific method of grouping (or classifying) insects, but it will help you to sort them out in your mind. Take notes on anything else that you notice about the insect. Does it have antennae? How long are they? Does the body have hairs on it? If so, then where? If it is an insect larva, does it have legs, and how many?

Make notes on the colours and patterns that you can see on the insect. Remember that insects change colour and shape as they grow into adults, and that the male of a species is sometimes a different colour from the female.

Quick check list

When you find an insect, look first to see whether it has wings. If it does, how many are there?

If it has one pair of wings, look at chart A.

If it has hard wing-cases, look at chart B.

If it has no wings, look at chart C.

If it has two pairs of wings, look at chart D.

A Insects with one pair of wings

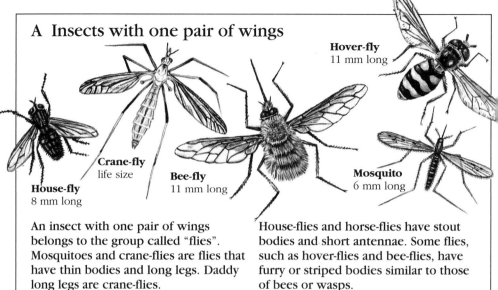

Hover-fly 11 mm long

Crane-fly life size

House-fly 8 mm long

Bee-fly 11 mm long

Mosquito 6 mm long

An insect with one pair of wings belongs to the group called "flies". Mosquitoes and crane-flies are flies that have thin bodies and long legs. Daddy long legs are crane-flies.

House-flies and horse-flies have stout bodies and short antennae. Some flies, such as hover-flies and bee-flies, have furry or striped bodies similar to those of bees or wasps.

B Insects with hard wing-cases

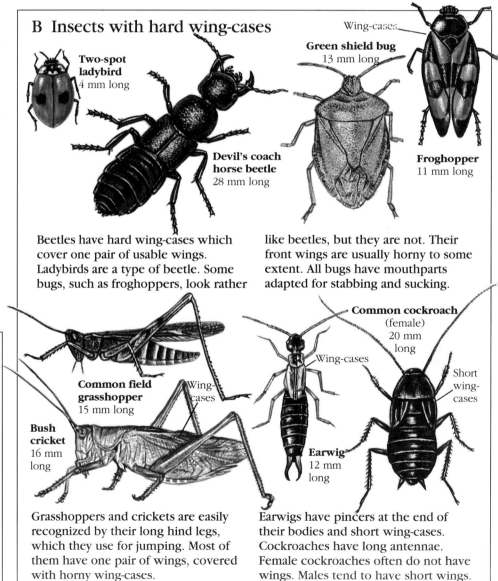

Wing-cases

Two-spot ladybird 4 mm long

Green shield bug 13 mm long

Devil's coach horse beetle 28 mm long

Froghopper 11 mm long

Beetles have hard wing-cases which cover one pair of usable wings. Ladybirds are a type of beetle. Some bugs, such as froghoppers, look rather

like beetles, but they are not. Their front wings are usually horny to some extent. All bugs have mouthparts adapted for stabbing and sucking.

Common cockroach (female) 20 mm long

Wing-cases

Short wing-cases

Common field grasshopper 15 mm long

Wing-cases

Bush cricket 16 mm long

Earwig 12 mm long

Grasshoppers and crickets are easily recognized by their long hind legs, which they use for jumping. Most of them have one pair of wings, covered with horny wing-cases.

Earwigs have pincers at the end of their bodies and short wing-cases. Cockroaches have long antennae. Female cockroaches often do not have wings. Males tend to have short wings.

C Insects without wings

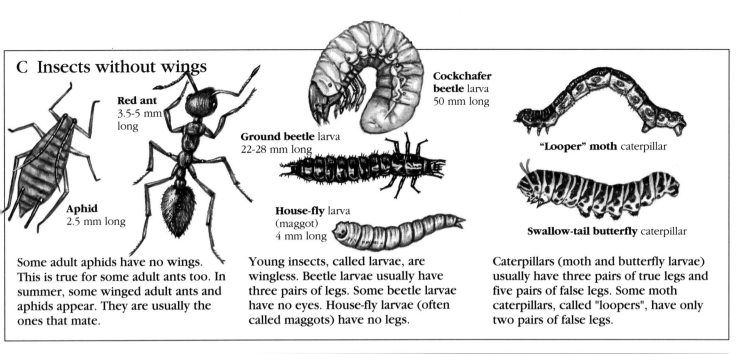

Red ant
3.5-5 mm
long

Aphid
2.5 mm long

Cockchafer beetle larva
50 mm long

Ground beetle larva
22-28 mm long

House-fly larva
(maggot)
4 mm long

"Looper" moth caterpillar

Swallow-tail butterfly caterpillar

Some adult aphids have no wings. This is true for some adult ants too. In summer, some winged adult ants and aphids appear. They are usually the ones that mate.

Young insects, called larvae, are wingless. Beetle larvae usually have three pairs of legs. Some beetle larvae have no eyes. House-fly larvae (often called maggots) have no legs.

Caterpillars (moth and butterfly larvae) usually have three pairs of true legs and five pairs of false legs. Some moth caterpillars, called "loopers", have only two pairs of false legs.

D Insects with two pairs of wings

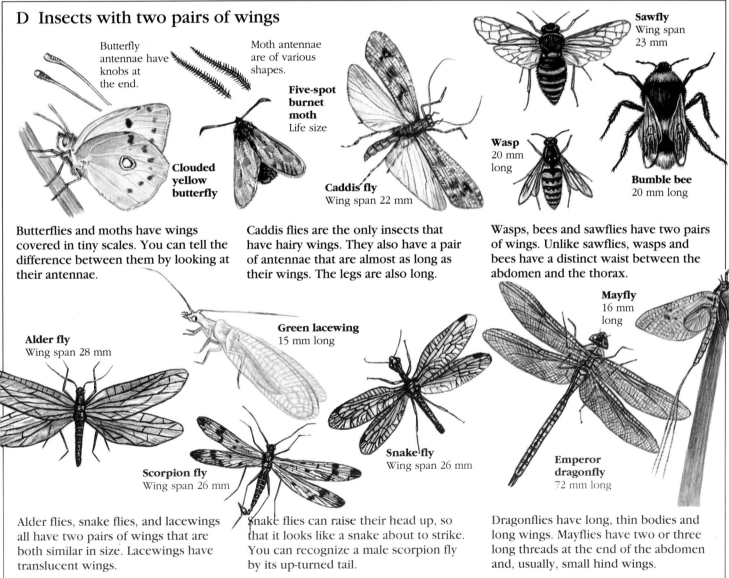

Butterfly antennae have knobs at the end.

Moth antennae are of various shapes.

Five-spot burnet moth
Life size

Clouded yellow butterfly

Caddis fly
Wing span 22 mm

Sawfly
Wing span 23 mm

Wasp
20 mm long

Bumble bee
20 mm long

Butterflies and moths have wings covered in tiny scales. You can tell the difference between them by looking at their antennae.

Caddis flies are the only insects that have hairy wings. They also have a pair of antennae that are almost as long as their wings. The legs are also long.

Wasps, bees and sawflies have two pairs of wings. Unlike sawflies, wasps and bees have a distinct waist between the abdomen and the thorax.

Alder fly
Wing span 28 mm

Green lacewing
15 mm long

Scorpion fly
Wing span 26 mm

Snake fly
Wing span 26 mm

Mayfly
16 mm
long

Emperor dragonfly
72 mm long

Alder flies, snake flies, and lacewings all have two pairs of wings that are both similar in size. Lacewings have translucent wings.

Snake flies can raise their head up, so that it looks like a snake about to strike. You can recognize a male scorpion fly by its up-turned tail.

Dragonflies have long, thin bodies and long wings. Mayflies have two or three long threads at the end of the abdomen and, usually, small hind wings.

Breeding, growing and changing

Most insects hatch from eggs. After they have hatched, they go through different stages of growth before becoming adults. Some young insects change shape completely before they are adult. Others just get bigger.

Insects such as crickets, earwigs, grasshoppers and bugs, hatch from the eggs looking like small adults. They have no wings when they hatch and are called nymphs. They moult several times, growing bigger each time. The nymph has small wing buds which expand into wings at the last moult.

Other insects change so much that when they hatch they do not look at all like the adults they will become.

The young of these types of insect, such as butterflies, moths, beetles, flies, ants and bees, are called larvae. A caterpillar is the larva of a moth or butterfly. Larvae moult several times as they grow.

When these larvae have grown to a certain size, they shed their skin for the last time and become pupae. Pupae do not feed and usually do not move. Inside the pupa, the body of the young insect slowly changes into an adult.

When the adult is ready to emerge, the pupal skin splits and the adult struggles out. It does not grow after this.

All insects have a soft skin at first, but this hardens and then cannot stretch. As they grow, insects have to change their skin by moulting.

A new skin grows under the old one. The old skin splits and the insect wriggles out, covered in its new, larger skin. Once the insect has become adult, it does not grow any more.

Dragonflies

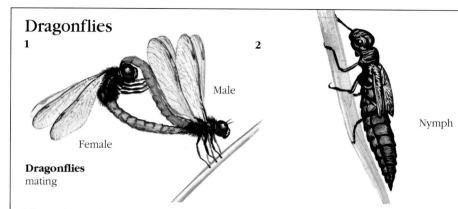

Dragonflies mating

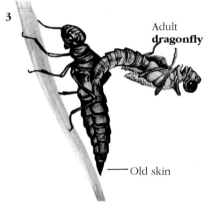

Female
Male

Nymph

These dragonflies are mating. The male holds on to the neck of the female. The female lays her eggs either straight on the water or on a water plant. Nymphs hatch from the eggs.

Dragonfly nymphs live in the water for two years or more. When they moult, they change colour to blend in with their surroundings. They crawl onto a stem before they moult into an adult.

3

Adult **dragonfly**

Old skin

4

Adult **dragonfly**

Old skin

Here, the adult dragonfly is emerging from the nymph. The skin of the nymph has split and first the head and then the thorax of the adult appear. The old skin still clings to the stem.

After a short rest, the adult dragonfly pulls its abdomen out of the old skin. Then it rests on the stem by hanging from its legs, while its body gains shape and the wings expand.

Grasshoppers

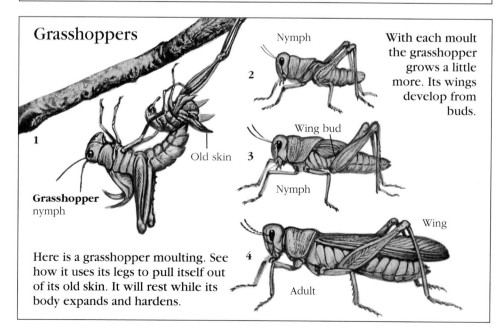

Nymph

2

With each moult the grasshopper grows a little more. Its wings develop from buds.

Old skin

1

Grasshopper nymph

Wing bud

3

Nymph

Wing

4

Adult

Here is a grasshopper moulting. See how it uses its legs to pull itself out of its old skin. It will rest while its body expands and hardens.

Mating

The adults of all types of insects mate with other insects of the same species. Then the females lay their eggs. Some are laid on stems, some are laid in or on the ground, and some in water.

Usually the eggs are laid on or near food that the larvae can feed on. The bluebottle eggs in the picture below have been laid on a dead animal. The larvae will feed on the animal when they hatch.

Lacewings lay their eggs on the end of a stalk that is made with special gum from the abdomen. It is thought that this method protects the eggs from ants that like to eat them.

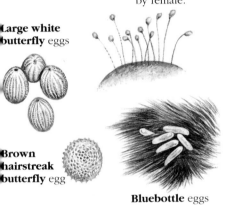

Lacewing eggs on stalks made of gum by female.

Large white butterfly eggs

Brown hairstreak butterfly egg

Bluebottle eggs

Female insects lay their eggs either singly, like the brown hairstreak butterfly, or in clusters, like the bluebottle and lacewing. A few insects leave the eggs once they are laid.

Gnats

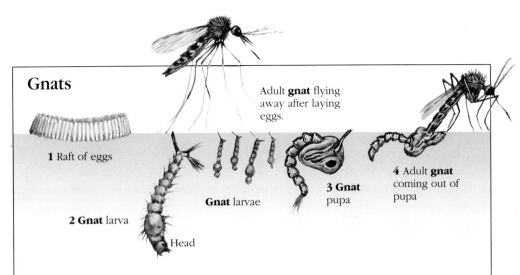

Adult **gnat** flying away after laying eggs.

1 Raft of eggs

Gnat larvae

2 Gnat larva

Head

3 Gnat pupa

4 Adult gnat coming out of pupa

Gnats lay their eggs in groups, which float like a raft on the water's surface (1). The larvae (2) hatch out, and hang from the surface, breathing air through a siphon. Each larva turns into a pupa (3), which also lives near the surface. When the adult has formed inside the pupa, the skin splits and it crawls out (4).

Butterflies

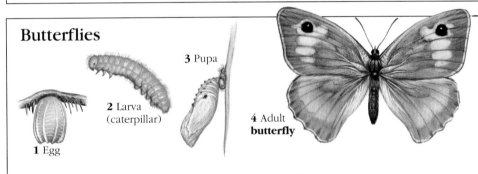

3 Pupa

2 Larva (caterpillar)

1 Egg

4 Adult butterfly

The meadow brown butterfly lays a single egg on grass (1). The caterpillar (2) hatches and spends the winter in this form. Early the next summer, it turns into a pupa (3).

Inside the pupa, or chrysalis, the body of the caterpillar breaks down and then becomes the body of the butterfly. This takes about four weeks. Then the pupa splits, and the adult emerges. It rests while its crumpled wings spread out and dry. Then it is ready to fly (4).

Stag beetles

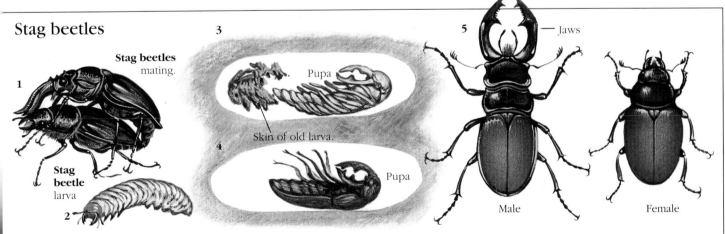

1

Stag beetles mating.

Stag beetle larva

2

3

Pupa

Skin of old larva.

4

Pupa

5

Jaws

Male

Female

After mating (1), the female stag beetle lays her eggs in the holes of rotten trees. The young larva (2) lives for three years, burrowing through the tree's soft wood. Then, the larva stops feeding, makes a pupal cell in the wood and becomes a pupa (3). It lies on its back to protect the newly-formed limbs until they harden (4). Then it emerges as an adult beetle (5). The males have large jaws that they use for fighting and to attract the females.

Insects in the garden

A good place to start a study of insects is your own garden. If you do not have a garden then look in a park or open green space. Make a chart of the insects you find there each month. Look under stones, on the bark of trees, on plants and grass, and among dead leaves. It is even worth looking in a garden shed.

Some insects spend the winter without moving or feeding. This is called hibernation. Make a note of where you find hibernating insects, but never disturb them.

1 On tree trunks

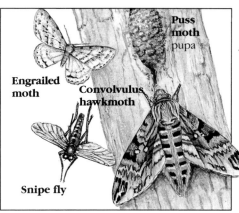

Moths, especially ones that are the colour of bark, rest on trees. In winter, look for pupae in bark crevices.

2 Under bark

Queen wasps and beetles sometimes hibernate under loose bark. Look for bark beetle tunnels in the bark.

6 In wood piles

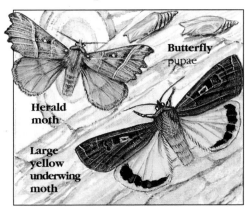

These insects hibernate in sheltered spots like wood piles in winter. Take great care not to disturb them.

7 On walls

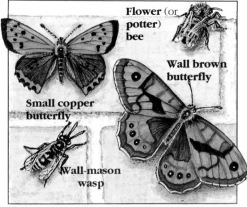

These insects can often be found on walls where they like to settle, particularly if the walls face the sun.

8 In the rubbish heap

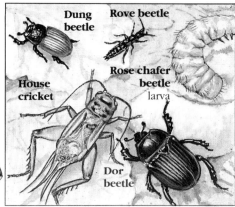

These insects feed on waste matter, such as animal droppings. You are most likely to find them in a rubbish heap.

9 Under stones

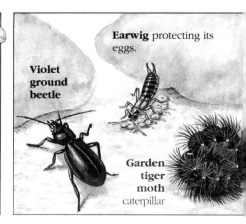

Lift up large stones and you will probably discover these insects. They like to live in dark, damp places.

3 On leaves and stems

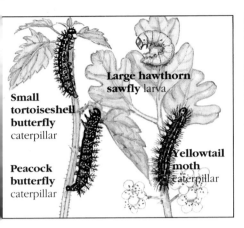

Small tortoiseshell butterfly caterpillar

Large hawthorn sawfly larva

Peacock butterfly caterpillar

Yellowtail moth caterpillar

Most caterpillars feed on leaves. Spot them in spring and summer, particularly on hedges and bushes.

4 Houses and sheds

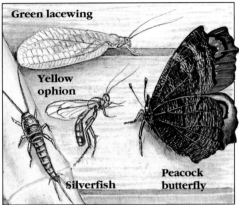

Green lacewing

Yellow ophion

Silverfish

Peacock butterfly

If you search a shed in winter, you may find a peacock butterfly or a green lacewing hibernating.

5 On grasses

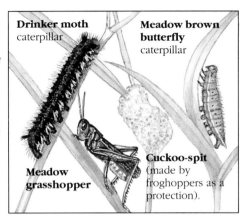

Drinker moth caterpillar

Meadow brown butterfly caterpillar

Meadow grasshopper

Cuckoo-spit (made by froghoppers as a protection).

Search carefully for insects on grasses. Many of them are green and blend in with surroundings, so are difficult to see.

The insect watcher's code

When looking for insects remember the insect watcher's code.

Always replace logs and stones exactly as you found them. They are often the homes of insects.

Search carefully and try not to damage flowers and twigs, and never peel the bark off trees.

You have a better chance of finding insects if you move slowly and quietly.

You can discover a lot just by waiting and watching.

10 In the soil

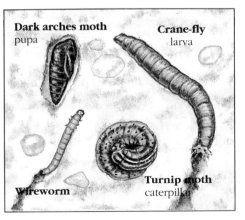

Dark arches moth pupa

Crane-fly larva

Wireworm

Turnip moth caterpillar

Some insects, such as these, live in the soil. You will have to dig to find them. The larvae feed on roots.

11 On flowers

Silver-washed fritillary

Hornet

In summer, you will see insects such as these feeding on the nectar and pollen of flowers.

12 On the ground

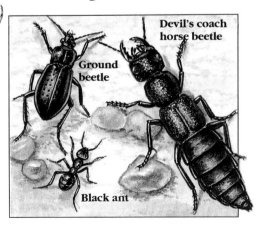

Devil's coach horse beetle

Ground beetle

Black ant

Watch ants and beetles scuttling over the ground in summer. See if you can follow them and spot where they go.

Insects in a tree

Thousands of different types of insect live in and on trees. You can make a study of the insects you find on one type of tree. The tree on this page is a common oak.

Try to choose a tree that stands on its own away from other trees. Make a note of how many kinds of insect you spot, where you find them on the tree and what the season is. See if you can identify them and discover some facts about them.

Is there a connection between the kinds of insect you find and the leaves, flowers or fruits on the tree? Compare the kinds of insect you find on your tree with those on other types of tree. Make a note of the differences and see if you can discover why each type of tree is better suited to certain insects.

Moth caterpillars

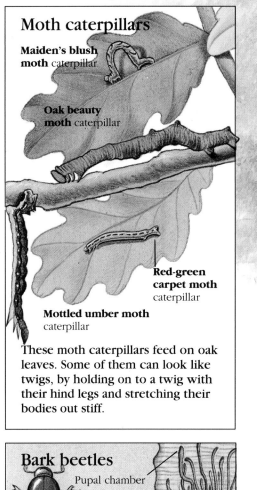

Maiden's blush moth caterpillar

Oak beauty moth caterpillar

Red-green carpet moth caterpillar

Mottled umber moth caterpillar

These moth caterpillars feed on oak leaves. Some of them can look like twigs, by holding on to a twig with their hind legs and stretching their bodies out stiff.

Greenfly

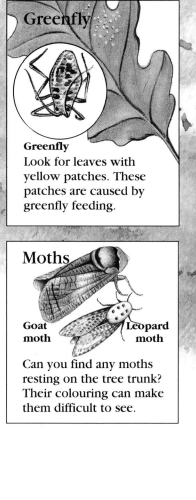

Greenfly
Look for leaves with yellow patches. These patches are caused by greenfly feeding.

Moths

Goat moth

Leopard moth

Can you find any moths resting on the tree trunk? Their colouring can make them difficult to see.

Weevils

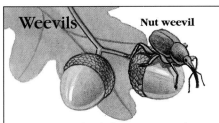

Nut weevil

In autumn, look for acorns with holes in them. These are where weevils have laid eggs. The female bores a tunnel into the acorn with her long nose and then places the egg at the end of it. The weevil larva feeds on the acorn.

Bark beetles

Pupal chamber

Oak bark beetle

Egg tunnel

Larvae feeding tunnels.

The female bark beetle bores a tunnel for her eggs. When the larvae hatch they bore tunnels at right angles to the main tunnel. They make a pupal chamber at the end, from which they emerge as adults.

Dig the soil a few metres from the tree and see what insects you can find there.

Look at rotting tree stumps as well as living trees. Note the different insects you find on each.

Green oak-roller

Green oak-roller moth

If disturbed, the caterpillar can lower itself on a silken thread.

The caterpillar hides and feeds inside an oak leaf, which it rolls over and binds with silk.

Carrion beetles

This four-spot carrion beetle feeds on green oak-roller moth caterpillars.

Beetles

Cockchafer beetle

Longhorn beetle

Cockchafer beetles eat the leaves of trees and other plants. Longhorn beetles lay their eggs in crevices in the bark.

Feeding

Common goldeneye lacewing

10-spot ladybird

Lacewings and ladybirds feed on aphids such as greenfly that live on oak trees.

Bugs

Capsid bug

There are many types of capsid bug. Some like to live on oak trees. They feed on the sap of the leaves, or on young acorns.

atch for birds ting insects on ees.

Look in the leaf litter on the ground beneath the tree for larvae and pupae.

Oak apple galls

Galls

Gall wasp (winged male) leaving gall.

In May, you can see oak apple galls like these. They are made by gall wasp larvae. The adult wasps emerge in mid-summer.

Moth larva

Common swift moth caterpillars feed on the young roots of trees, and other plants. They pupate in the soil.

Beetle larva

Cockchafer larvae live in the soil for at least three years. They feed on the roots of trees and are very destructive to young trees.

Gall wasps

Gall

Gall wasp (wingless female)

Gall wasps lay their eggs in oak roots. Galls form with larvae inside. Wingless females emerge and crawl up the tree to lay their eggs in the buds, which swell into oak apples.

Pond insects

The best time of year to spot all these pond insects is in early summer. This is the time when the dragonflies and other flying insects change from being nymphs, larvae and pupae living in the water, to adults.

Look in different places around the pond. Watch the insects that fly over the pond and those that are on the surface. Search among the water weeds and use your net to find insects in the water.

Banded agrion damselfly

Mayfly

What you need

Take a pond net for catching insects that live in the water or on the surface. You can use a plastic sieve in shallow water.

You also need a shallow white dish to tip your catch into, and a teaspoon for putting it into a screw-topped container. A trowel is useful for scooping up mud by the pond's edge.

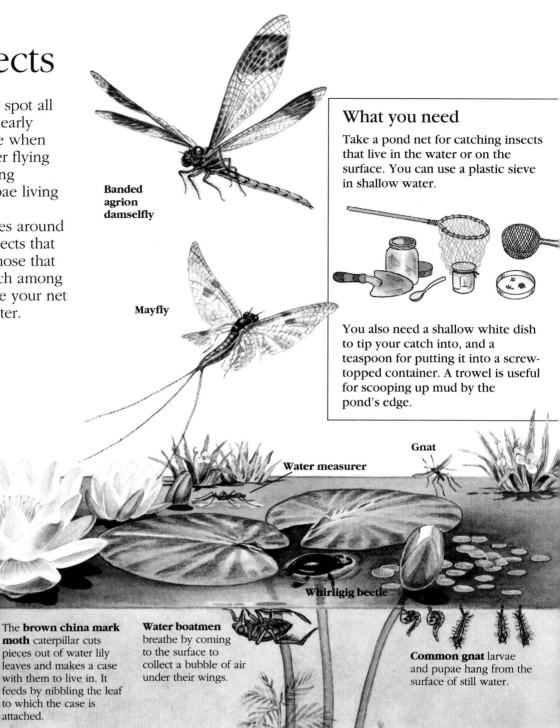

Gnat

Water measurer

Whirligig beetle

The **brown china mark moth** caterpillar cuts pieces out of water lily leaves and makes a case with them to live in. It feeds by nibbling the leaf to which the case is attached.

Water boatmen breathe by coming to the surface to collect a bubble of air under their wings.

Common gnat larvae and pupae hang from the surface of still water.

The **great diving beetle** is a very powerful swimmer. It uses its hind legs like oars. It eats snails, small fish and tadpoles.

Damselfly nymphs live completely in the water. They breathe through three gills at the end of the abdomen.

Dragonfly nymphs shoot out a long pincer-like "mask" to catch fish and other insects.

Mayfly nymph

Make a pond net

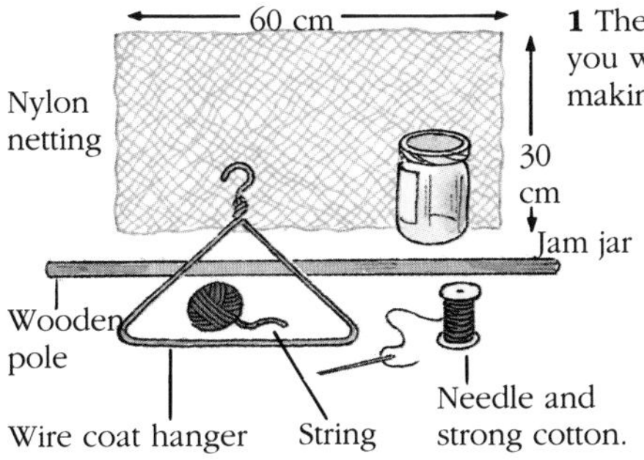

1 These are the things you will need for making a pond net.

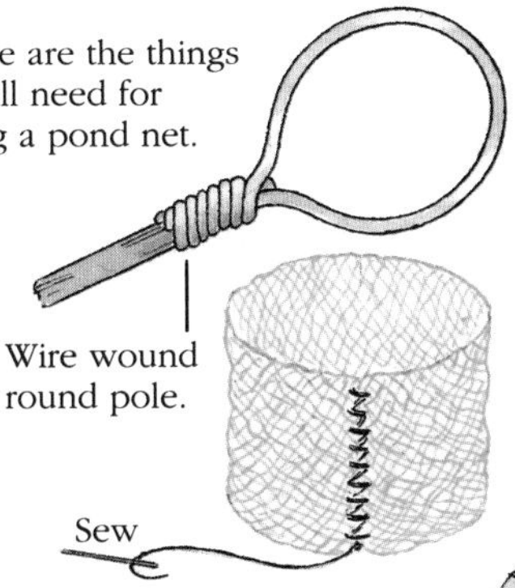

60 cm

Nylon netting

30 cm

Jam jar

Wooden pole

Wire coat hanger   String   Needle and strong cotton.

2 Take the coat hanger and bend it into a hoop with pliers and wind the ends round the pole. Sew the edges of the netting together.

Wire wound round pole.

Sew

3 Sew the netting to the wire frame as shown in the picture above.

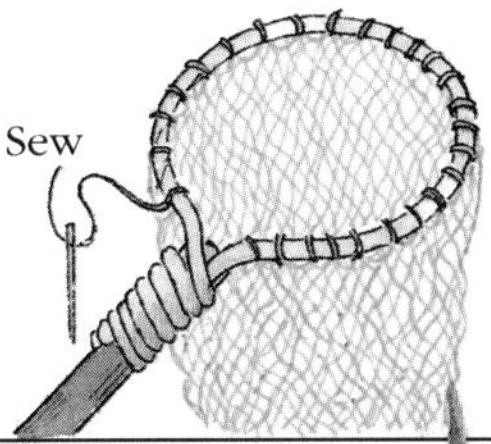

Sew

4 Now fix the jar to the netting with string. Then tie the string over the wire on the pole to strengthen it.

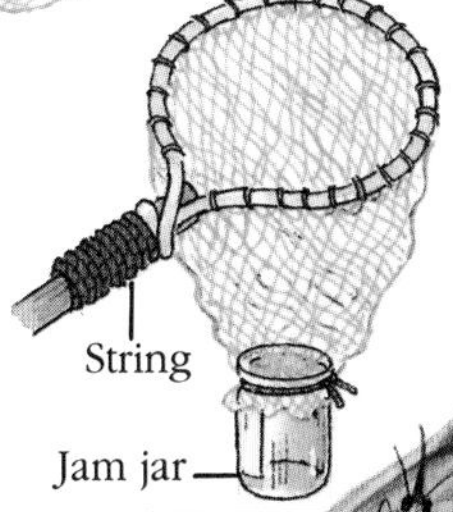

String

Jam jar

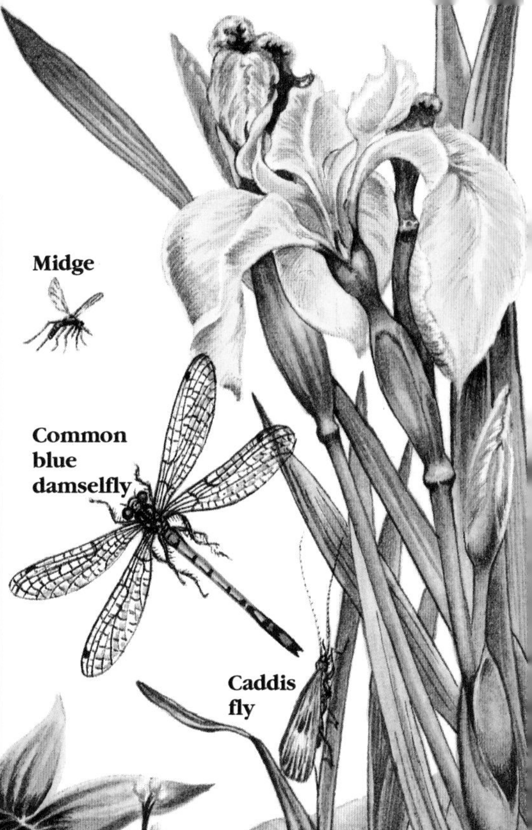

Midge

Common blue damselfly

Caddis fly

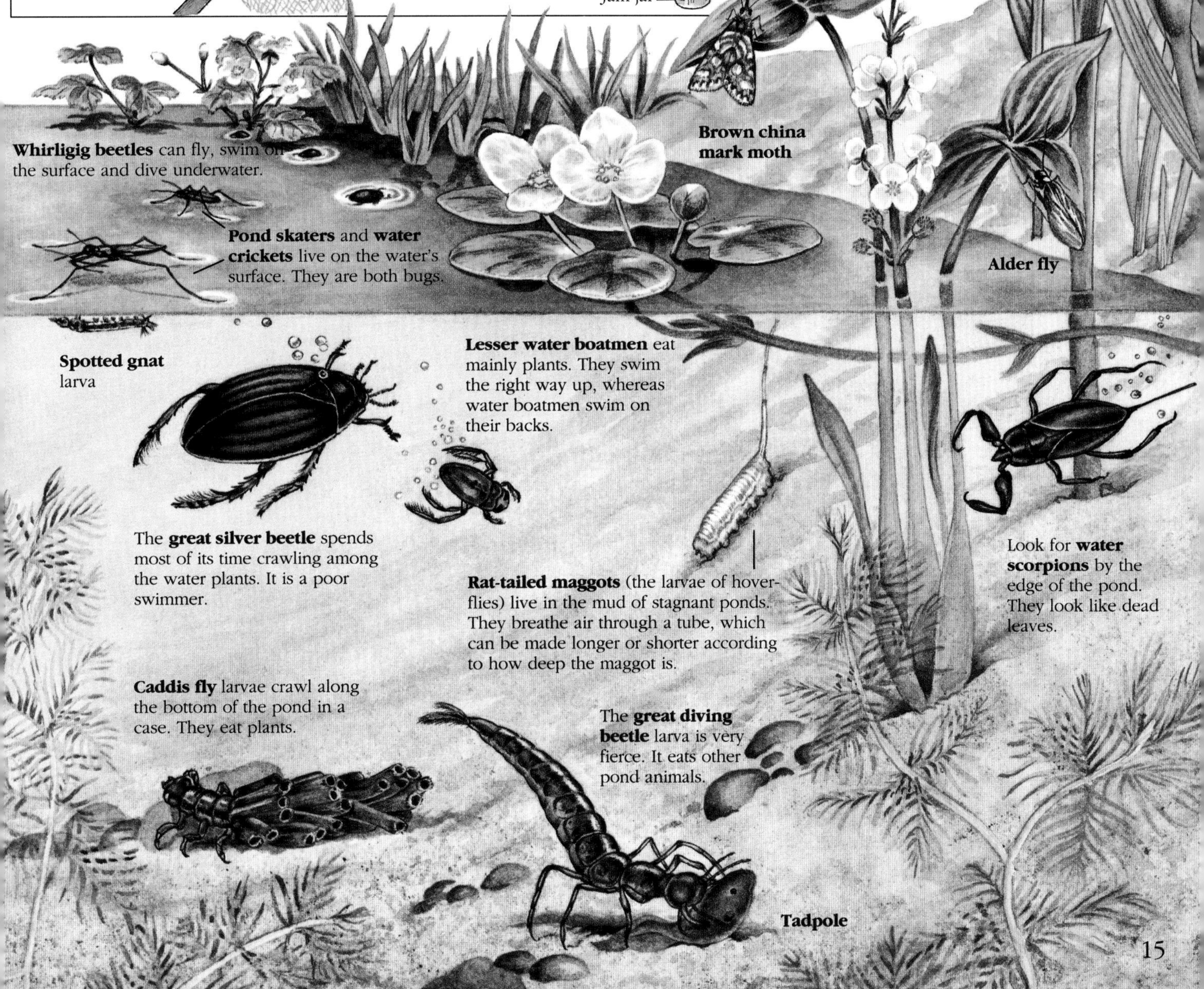

Brown china mark moth

Alder fly

Whirligig beetles can fly, swim on the surface and dive underwater.

Pond skaters and **water crickets** live on the water's surface. They are both bugs.

Spotted gnat larva

Lesser water boatmen eat mainly plants. They swim the right way up, whereas water boatmen swim on their backs.

Look for **water scorpions** by the edge of the pond. They look like dead leaves.

The **great silver beetle** spends most of its time crawling among the water plants. It is a poor swimmer.

Rat-tailed maggots (the larvae of hover-flies) live in the mud of stagnant ponds. They breathe air through a tube, which can be made longer or shorter according to how deep the maggot is.

Caddis fly larvae crawl along the bottom of the pond in a case. They eat plants.

The **great diving beetle** larva is very fierce. It eats other pond animals.

Tadpole

15

Insect senses

Insects do not sense things in the same way that we do. They do not have a nose for smelling. However, insects can feel, smell and taste with their antennae. Some can also taste with their feet. The hairs on an insect's body help it to feel.

Most insects have hairs on their bodies. These hairs are stiff and they are connected to nerve cells. The insect can feel every movement of the hairs.

Simple eyes

The antennae are an important sense organ. They are sensitive to heat and damp, as well as being used for smelling and tasting. Only parts of the bluebottle's antennae are shown. The main parts are in front of the head.

Compound eye

Bluebottle (or **blow-fly**)

Insects have two kinds of eyes - simple eyes, called ocelli, and compound eyes. The compound eyes are made up of thousands of separate lenses. Insects do not focus their eyes in the same way that we do. They can, however, detect even the slightest movement. Some insects can see forwards, backwards, and downwards all at the same time.

Some insects, such as butterflies, bees and bluebottles, can taste with their feet. When they land on something sweet, they immediately put out their proboscis and start feeding.

How grasshoppers and crickets "sing"

Male grasshoppers and crickets can "sing" by rubbing together two parts of their body. Crickets rub together roughened parts on their wings. Both male and female crickets have ears on their front legs. The song of some types of cricket can be heard 900 m away.

Grasshoppers rub their legs, which have a row of tiny "pegs" on them, against the hard vein on their forewings. Each type of grasshopper makes a different sound. They sing to attract females or to compete against a rival. Male and female grasshoppers have ears on the first pair of legs or on the side of the abdomen.

Grasshoppers rub their legs against a hard vein on their wings.

Legs move up and down.

Roughened parts

Wings move towards each other and out again.

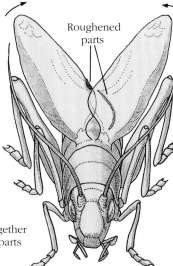

Crickets rub together two roughened parts on their wings.

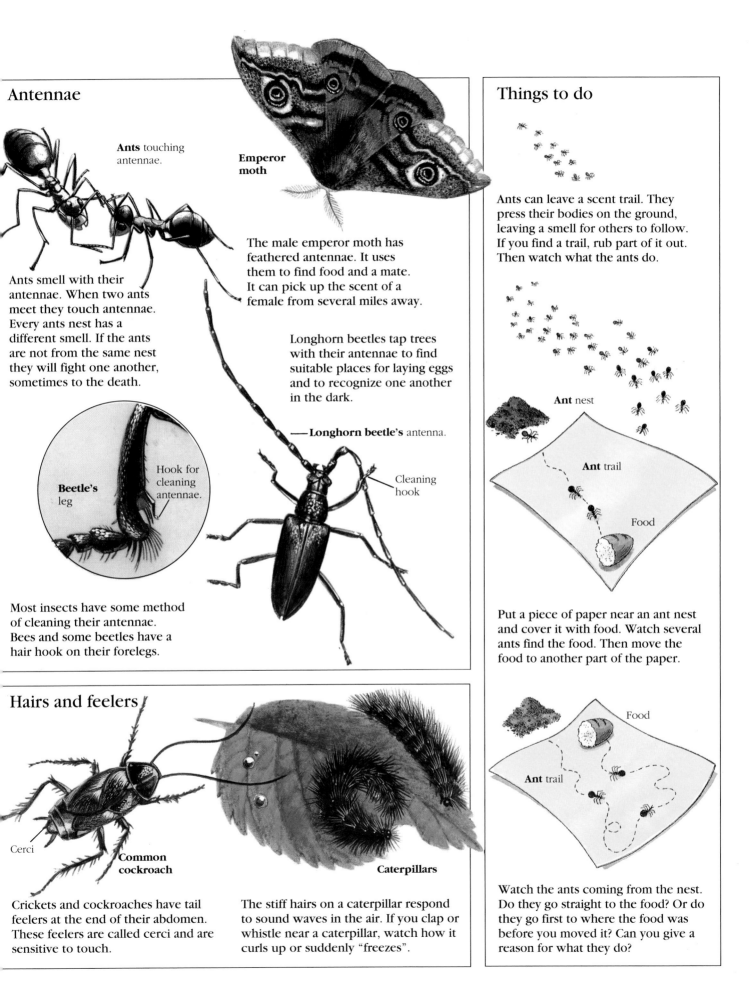

Antennae

Ants touching antennae.

Emperor moth

Ants smell with their antennae. When two ants meet they touch antennae. Every ants nest has a different smell. If the ants are not from the same nest they will fight one another, sometimes to the death.

The male emperor moth has feathered antennae. It uses them to find food and a mate. It can pick up the scent of a female from several miles away.

Longhorn beetles tap trees with their antennae to find suitable places for laying eggs and to recognize one another in the dark.

—**Longhorn beetle's** antenna.

Hook for cleaning antennae.

Beetle's leg

Cleaning hook

Most insects have some method of cleaning their antennae. Bees and some beetles have a hair hook on their forelegs.

Hairs and feelers

Cerci

Common cockroach

Caterpillars

Crickets and cockroaches have tail feelers at the end of their abdomen. These feelers are called cerci and are sensitive to touch.

The stiff hairs on a caterpillar respond to sound waves in the air. If you clap or whistle near a caterpillar, watch how it curls up or suddenly "freezes".

Things to do

Ants can leave a scent trail. They press their bodies on the ground, leaving a smell for others to follow. If you find a trail, rub part of it out. Then watch what the ants do.

Ant nest

Ant trail

Food

Put a piece of paper near an ant nest and cover it with food. Watch several ants find the food. Then move the food to another part of the paper.

Food

Ant trail

Watch the ants coming from the nest. Do they go straight to the food? Or do they go first to where the food was before you moved it? Can you give a reason for what they do?

Watching insects move

Many insects have their own particular way of moving. If you learn to recognize these different movements, then you will be able to identify the insects more easily. Insects that walk or run usually have long, thin legs. Insects that dig, such as dor beetles, have forelegs that are shorter but stronger than the other two pairs. Insects that jump or swim often have specially developed hind-legs. Compare the way different insects fly. Wasps, flies and bees flap their wings faster than butterflies when they fly.

Flying

Look at the different shapes of insects' wings, and watch how fast or slowly they fly. Look to see if they have one pair of wings or two.

Halteres

Flies have only one pair of wings. Instead of hind wings they have two knobs, called halteres. These help the insect to balance.

When a **beetle** flies it holds up its stiff wing-cases, to let its wings move easily. When it lands it folds its wings back under the wing-cases.

Wing-case

Cockchafer beetle

Jumping

Grasshopper jumping

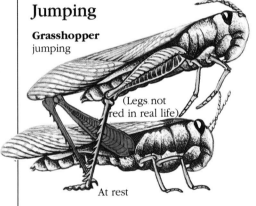

(Legs not red in real life)

At rest

The grasshopper's powerful, long back legs with their strong thighs help it to leap. As it straightens its legs, the grasshopper is propelled into the air.

Swimming

Water boatman

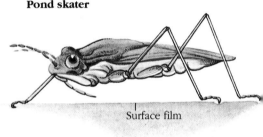

Hairs

Some underwater swimmers have flattened hind legs, fringed with long hairs. They use these legs like oars, moving them both together.

Walking on water

Pond skater

Surface film

Heavy objects break the surface film on water and sink. A pond skater is light and has long spread-out legs. It walks on the surface without breaking the film.

Digging

Mole cricket burrowing

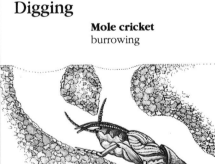

Insects that burrow often have short, wide front legs. These legs are flattened and can have teeth, which helps the insect dig into the soil.

How caterpillars move

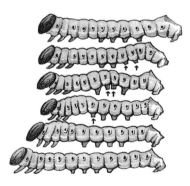

Caterpillars have three pairs of walking legs and up to five pairs of false legs. All caterpillars, except "loopers", walk by moving each pair of false legs in turn.

Looper caterpillars

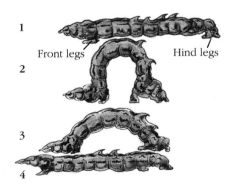

1

Front legs   Hind legs

2

3

4

A "looper" caterpillar moves forward by bringing forward its hind legs (1, 2) causing the body to arch, and then stretching out its front legs (3, 4).

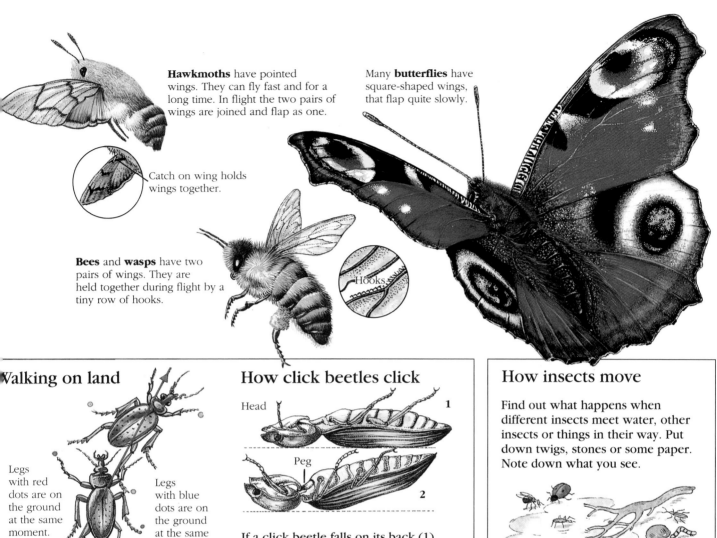

Hawkmoths have pointed wings. They can fly fast and for a long time. In flight the two pairs of wings are joined and flap as one.

Many **butterflies** have square-shaped wings, that flap quite slowly.

Catch on wing holds wings together.

Bees and **wasps** have two pairs of wings. They are held together during flight by a tiny row of hooks.

Hooks.

Walking on land

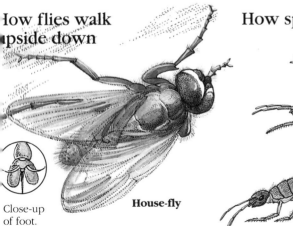

Legs with red dots are on the ground at the same moment.

Legs with blue dots are on the ground at the same moment.

Insects that walk often have long thin legs, which are all alike. They walk by moving three legs at a time and balancing on the other three.

How flies walk upside down

Close-up of foot.

House-fly

House-flies have sticky, hairy pads on their feet. Because the fly is so light, the grip of the pads is strong enough to hold it on almost any surface.

How click beetles click

Head

1

Peg

2

If a click beetle falls on its back (1), it arches its body until only its head and tail touch the ground. A peg on its thorax makes it double up (2). Its wing-cases hit the ground and the beetle is thrown into the air, with a "clicking" sound.

How springtails jump

1 At rest

2 Jumping

Fork

3 Landing

Springtails cannot fly, but they can jump. Their forked tail, which folds under the body, flicks down on the ground and throws the insect forward.

How insects move

Find out what happens when different insects meet water, other insects or things in their way. Put down twigs, stones or some paper. Note down what you see.

See whether insects move at the same speed on different kinds of surface. Compare how they move on soil, grass and wood.

Smoke the top side of a plate over a candle. Be very careful and do not hold the plate over the flame for too long as it may crack. When it has cooled, put the plate on the ground and watch insects move over it. Look at the different tracks made in the soot with a pocket lens and see what patterns each insect makes.

Watching insects feed

Insects feed on almost every kind of animal and plant. Some insects, such as cockroaches, will eat almost anything, but most insects feed only on one particular kind of food. There are insects that feed on cork, paper, clothes, ink, cigarettes, carpets, flour - and even shoe-polish.

The diet of an insect may change at different stages in its life. Most insects eat either plants or animals. However, some insects eat only animals when they are larvae and eat only plants when they are adults, or vice versa.

Insects that eat plants are called herbivores. More than half of all insects eat plants. Some feed on the leaves, flowers or seeds of plants, others bite the roots or suck the sap from inside plant stems. Some insects feed on nectar and pollen. You can find out more about this on page 22.

Some insects feed on animals smaller than themselves, or suck the blood from larger ones, sometimes after paralyzing or killing them. Female mosquitoes and horse-flies usually need to have a meal of mammal's blood before they can produce eggs. Many insects feed inside the bodies of other animals, and live there all the time. They are called parasites.

Some insects are called scavengers. They eat any decaying material that they find in the soil, such as animals that are already dead, and rotting plants. They also feed on the dung of animals. Flea larvae eat the droppings of adult fleas, as well as dirt and the skin fragments that come from the animal they are living on.

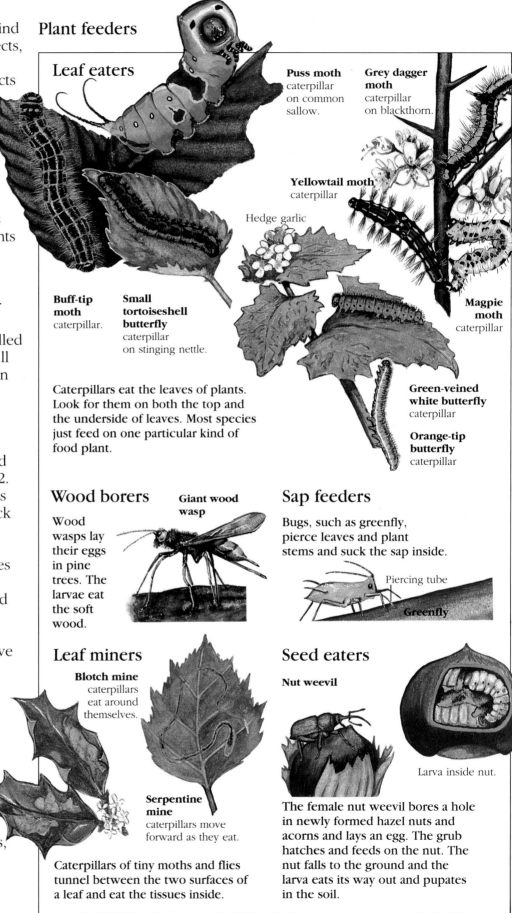

Plant feeders

Leaf eaters

Puss moth caterpillar on common sallow.

Grey dagger moth caterpillar on blackthorn.

Yellowtail moth caterpillar

Hedge garlic

Magpie moth caterpillar

Buff-tip moth caterpillar.

Small tortoiseshell butterfly caterpillar on stinging nettle.

Green-veined white butterfly caterpillar

Orange-tip butterfly caterpillar

Caterpillars eat the leaves of plants. Look for them on both the top and the underside of leaves. Most species just feed on one particular kind of food plant.

Wood borers

Giant wood wasp

Wood wasps lay their eggs in pine trees. The larvae eat the soft wood.

Sap feeders

Bugs, such as greenfly, pierce leaves and plant stems and suck the sap inside.

Piercing tube

Greenfly

Leaf miners

Blotch mine caterpillars eat around themselves.

Serpentine mine caterpillars move forward as they eat.

Caterpillars of tiny moths and flies tunnel between the two surfaces of a leaf and eat the tissues inside.

Seed eaters

Nut weevil

Larva inside nut.

The female nut weevil bores a hole in newly formed hazel nuts and acorns and lays an egg. The grub hatches and feeds on the nut. The nut falls to the ground and the larva eats its way out and pupates in the soil.

Insect mouthparts

Insects either suck liquids, or bite and chew solid food. Insects that suck have a hollow tube, called a proboscis. Bees, butterflies and moths suck nectar from inside flowers. Bugs can pierce plant stems and suck the sap inside. Mosquitoes pierce the skin of animals or humans and suck their blood.

Insects that bite and chew have three different pairs of mouthparts - a large pair called mandibles, a smaller pair called maxillae and a third pair which are joined together to form a kind of lower lip.

Green mirid bug

Piercing proboscis

Bee

Proboscis

Mosquito

Antenna

Mouthparts (usually in a bundle).

Sucking tube

Beetle

Mandibles — Maxillae

Coiled proboscis

Butterfly

Sucking pad

House-fly

Animal feeders

Aphid eaters

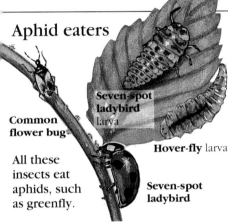

Seven-spot ladybird larva

Hover-fly larva

Common flower bug

Seven-spot ladybird

All these insects eat aphids, such as greenfly.

Wasps

Some wasps sting caterpillars, take them to their nest and lay eggs upon them.

Red-banded sand wasp

Dragonflies

Some dragonflies are often called "hawkers" because they fly so fast and overpower other insects.

Tiger beetles

Tiger beetles run fast and catch other insects with their strong mandibles. Their larvae burrow holes in the sand and hide there to wait for prey.

Larva in burrow.—

Mosquitoes

Mosquitoes usually fly by night. The female sucks blood. The male sucks nectar from flowers.

Skin

Robber-flies

Robber-flies pounce on insects in the air and suck them dry.

Scavengers

Blow-flies

Blow-flies lay their eggs on meat. The larvae (maggots) eat the meat when they hatch.

Bluebottle (Blow-fly)

Meat —

Dor beetles

Balls of dung.

Eggs

Dor beetles dig tunnels under cow dung. The female lays her eggs in chambers. The larvae feed on balls of dung.

Burying beetles

Burying beetles dig a hole and pull dead animals underground. They lay their eggs near the corpse.

Insects and flowers

Many insects visit flowers for food. Moths and butterflies feed on nectar, a sweet liquid found inside most flowers. Bees collect pollen, the yellow dust inside flowers, as well as nectar.

Flowers do not need the nectar they produce, except to attract insects. The insects help the flowers to make new seeds. Most insects that visit flowers are hairy. When they feed on a flower the hairs become dusted with pollen from the ripe stamens (the male parts inside a flower). Then the insects visit other flowers of the same species, and some of the sticky pollen may be accidentally brushed off onto the stigmas (the female parts of the flower).

This is called pollination. New seeds start to grow only when a flower has been pollinated.

Flowers that attract insects usually have a strong scent and can be brightly coloured. Insects do not see colours as we do. Flowers that look one colour to us, such as the yellow tormentil, appear white with dark centres to an insect.

Nectar guides

Foxglove
Spots

Tiger lily

Blue primrose

Pansy

Field bindweed
Lines

Some flowers that insects visit have lines or spots on their petals, pointing to where the nectar is. These patterns are called nectar guides. Flowers that have nectar guides are usually those where nectar is deeply hidden.

Adult bees feed only on nectar. Wasps feed on sweet liquids, such as from a ripe plum, as well as on nectar. Bees make honey from the nectar they gather. Bee larvae feed on pollen mixed with the honey. Young queen bees are fed on a richer type of this food, called royal jelly. Wasp larvae have a few meals of nectar and then feed on insects captured and brought to them by the adults.

Pollination

Pollen rubs off the stamen onto bee's body as it collects nectar.

Stigma
Stamen
Nectar

On the next flower, the stigma is in a different position. Pollen rubs off onto it.

Stigma
Stamen
Nectar

Wasp

Michaelmas daisy

Common blue butterfly

Look for drone-flies on hogweed and wild carrot.

Hogweed

Drone-fly

22

Feeding on flowers

Garden chafer beetle

Beetles have mouthparts that bite and chew. Nectar feeding beetles cannot suck nectar like bees. This means they only feed on flowers where the nectar is easy to get at.

Hover fly

Proboscis

Some flies that suck nectar look like bees. They have a hairy body and their tongue, called a proboscis, is longer than that of other flies. Look for them on wide-open flowers.

Long proboscis

Hawkmoth

Most moths fly at dusk or at night. They are attracted to pale-coloured flowers that can be seen easily in the dark. Nectar is stored deep inside the flower, so a moth must have a long proboscis.

Watch how a butterfly extends its long proboscis into a flower, as soon as it lands. Butterflies feed from bright, scented flowers.

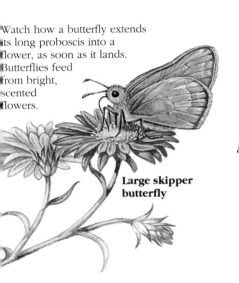

Large skipper butterfly

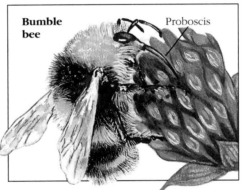

Bumble bee

Proboscis

Bees only gather nectar from one species of flower at a time. Watch this for yourself. Follow a single bee from flower to flower. Can you identify the type of flower it visits? Make a list of the different types of flower that bees visit.

Pollen on legs.

Honey bee

Honey bees collect nectar and pollen. Nectar is sucked up through the proboscis. Pollen is packed on the hind legs and held there by stiff bristles. This pollen can help to make seeds in the next flower the bee visits.

Make a butterfly garden

Try growing some of these plants to attract butterflies. Butterflies feed on flowers, and some lay eggs on weeds such as nettles. Keep a monthly record of the kinds of flowers that different insects visit. Note the shape and colour of each flower and whether it has a strong scent. Find out which flowers seem to attract most insects.

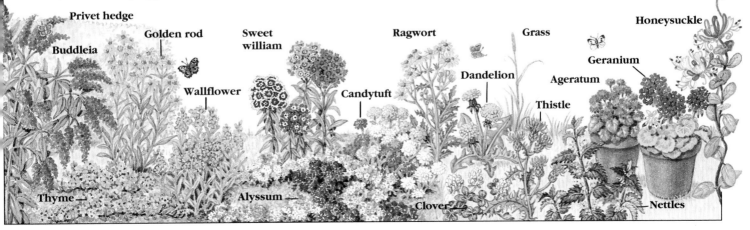

Privet hedge

Golden rod

Buddleia

Wallflower

Sweet william

Candytuft

Ragwort

Dandelion

Thistle

Grass

Ageratum

Geranium

Honeysuckle

Thyme

Alyssum

Clover

Nettles

Ants and bees

Ants and bees are "social" insects. This means that they live in colonies of sometimes thousands of insects. The food and work in the colony is shared.

In each colony there is a queen, who is the only egg-laying female. Then there are the males, called drones, whose only job is to mate with the queen. The third type of insect are undeveloped females. These are called workers and they do all the work in the colony. Each worker has a particular task, either to collect food and to care for the eggs and larvae, or to guard the nest.

An ant nest

Ants make their nests by burrowing in sand or soil. Some worker ants have the special job of building and repairing the nest. A gland in the ant's jaw produces a sticky liquid which can help to "cement" the nest together. Ant nests are made up of a network of chambers and passages. The queen has her own chamber and there are separate chambers for eggs, larvae and pupae. Other chambers are used for storing food or for rubbish. The entrance of the nest is closed at night, during rain or when it is very cold. In winter, the worker ants make the nest go deeper below ground.

How ants are born

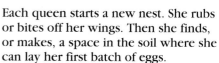

Queen **ant** (having shed one wing).

Queen laying eggs.

In warm summer weather, the winged males and queens leave the nest on a mating flight. After mating, the males die. The queen flies to the ground.

Each queen starts a new nest. She rubs or bites off her wings. Then she finds, or makes, a space in the soil where she can lay her first batch of eggs.

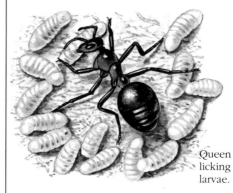

Queen licking larvae.

Worker ants picking up larvae.

The queen feeds the larvae with her own saliva. Later they become worker ants and take over the job of looking after the nest and the eggs.

Now the queen does nothing but lay more eggs. Workers feed the larvae and lick them clean. They cut the pupae open to let the new ants climb out.

Food

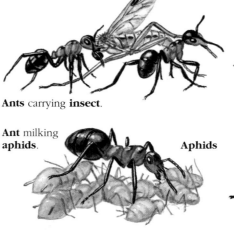

Ants carrying **insect**.

Ant milking **aphids**.

Aphids

Some ants go out collecting small insects, worms and other food. Others lick the sweet honeydew that aphids on nearby plants produce.

Defence and cleaning

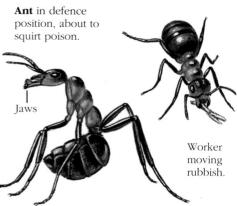

Ant in defence position, about to squirt poison.

Jaws

Worker moving rubbish.

Worker ants guard the nest. Ants keep their nest very clean, moving rubbish out of the nest or into special chambers. Some ants can squirt poison at an enemy.

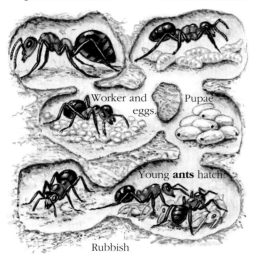

Queen in chamber.

Worker and larvae.

Worker and eggs.

Pupae

Young **ants** hatch.

Rubbish

Honey bees

Drone

There is only one queen in each hive.

Worker

These are three different kinds of honey bee that you will find in a bee hive. The only honey bees you will see flying around are the workers. The others stay only in the hive.

The honeycomb

This is what the inside of a honey bee's comb looks like. It is made of six-sided wax cells. Those near the outside are for breeding drones and for storing honey. Those in the middle are brood cells for worker bees. Pollen is packed in cells next to the brood cells. Queen bee larvae have special cells.

The workers do all the jobs. Young workers clean out cells, then as they get older, they feed the larvae, build new cells and make honey. Later they collect nectar and pollen.

Royal jelly

Queen bee larva

Capped **queen cell** cut away to show larva inside.

Uncapped **brood cell** containing egg or larva of worker bee.

Brood cell, capped, with larva inside.

Uncapped **honey cell**.

Cell containing **honey** and **pollen**, which is food for the larvae.

Pollen cell

Cell filled with **honey** and capped with **wax**.

How a bee grows

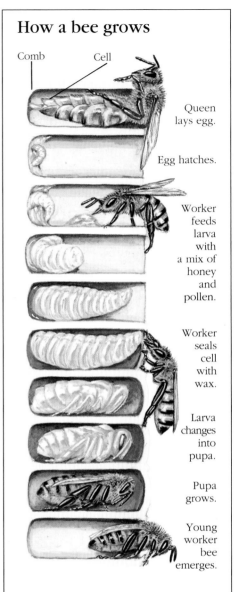

Comb   Cell

Queen lays egg.

Egg hatches.

Worker feeds larva with a mix of honey and pollen.

Worker seals cell with wax.

Larva changes into pupa.

Pupa grows.

Young worker bee emerges.

The queen lays one egg in each cell. After three days the eggs hatch. The worker bees feed the larvae on a mixture of honey and pollen. Queen bee larvae are fed on a rich mixture of honey and pollen and some other substances, called royal jelly.

After six days the larvae are large and fat and fill their cells. Worker bees seal the cells with wax made in the bodies of the bees. Inside the cells the larvae pupate. Two weeks later the young bees eat through the seal of wax and emerge fully grown. Before the young worker bees fly from the hive, they sometimes have the special job of keeping the air fresh in the hive by fanning their wings.

Collecting and keeping insects

When you find an insect, out in the garden or in some other place, put it in a small tin. Also place in the tin a piece of the plant on which you found the insect. The plant will give the insect some food and help you to identify it.

Number each tin. Write the numbers in your notebook and, against each one, write a description of the insect and where you found it. Was it in a dry or damp place, a sunny or a shady place?

If you want to keep your insects, when you get home you must put them in a place that is as similar as possible to their natural surroundings. You will need containers that are big enough to hold sufficient food and give the insects some room to move around. It is best to use glass or clear plastic containers, then you can see what is happening inside.

It is usually a good idea to put some sand or soil at the bottom, with a stone and some plants. Keep the containers in a cool place away from the sunlight, but not in a draught.

Make sure you have a good supply of fresh food and change it each day. Most caterpillars have their own particular food plant and will not eat anything else. There is no point in collecting them unless you can give them the right food supply.

Look at the insects in your "zoo" every day and record any changes that you see. You could keep a note of how much caterpillars eat and their length, or describe what happens to them when they pupate. See if you can spot different types of behaviour in different types of caterpillars. Watch how they move and eat.

Collecting crawling insects

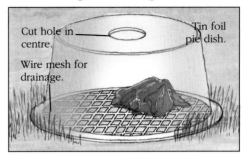

Try making a trap like this. Put bait, such as a piece of meat, in the trap to attract insects. A good place to put the trap is at the bottom of a hedge.

You could also make a pitfall trap. Try different baits, such as jam, raw meat, fruit or beer. Keep a record of the insects that are attracted by each bait.

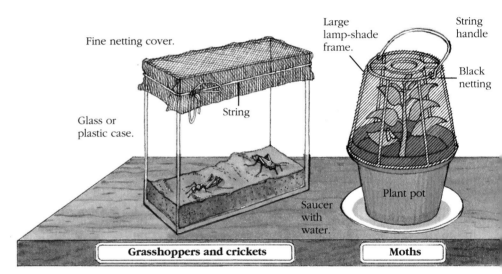

Grasshoppers and crickets

Moths

In late summer, you may find crickets and grasshoppers. Keep them in a large glass case or jar with sand in the bottom. Put in fresh grass every other day.

Make a moth cage. Keep it out of the sun and in hot weather spray it with water. If you want the moths to breed, put in the right plant for the larvae to feed on.

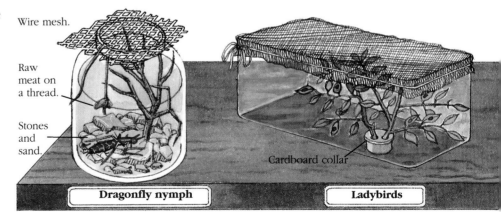

Dragonfly nymph

Ladybirds

Keep a dragonfly nymph on its own in a large jam jar and feed it on raw meat. Put in an upright stick for the nymph to cling to when it sheds its skin.

Keep ladybirds in a large case to give them room to fly. They feed on greenfly, often found on rose shoots. Cut off the whole shoot and keep it in water.

Sugaring

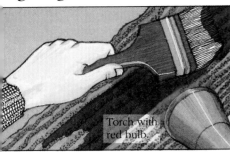

Torch with a red bulb.

You can attract moths by "sugaring". Paint tree trunks or posts at dusk with a mixture of black treacle and rum or beer. Warm, still evenings are best.

Lights

Light-traps are used to catch insects. Other lights, such as from a lamp, also attract them. How many can you find that are attracted to light in this way.

Remember

It is easy to collect insects, but remember that they are very fragile. Handle them as little as possible and do not collect more than you need to study.

If you keep the insects for a few days to study, make sure you supply them with a piece of the plant on which you found them.

Never collect a rare or protected species.

Once you have finished looking at them, take the insects back to the place where you found them. Let flying insects go at dusk so that birds or cats do not attack and kill them.

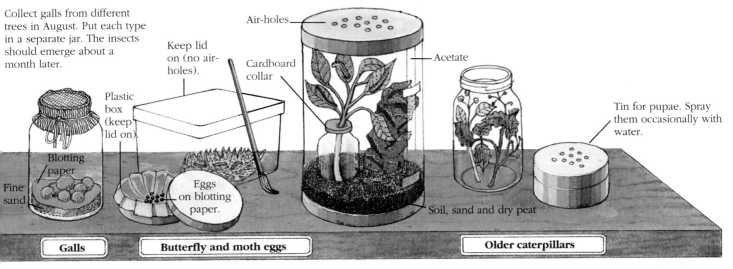

Collect galls from different trees in August. Put each type in a separate jar. The insects should emerge about a month later.

Keep lid on (no air-holes).

Plastic box (keep lid on).

Blotting paper

Fine sand

Eggs on blotting paper.

Air-holes

Cardboard collar

Acetate

Soil, sand and dry peat

Tin for pupae. Spray them occasionally with water.

Galls

Butterfly and moth eggs

Older caterpillars

Collect butterfly or moth eggs in small boxes. When the caterpillars hatch, put them in another box and give them a new leaf of their food plant each day.

To make a container for older caterpillars, roll up some acetate and fix it with sticky tape. Put one half of a tin on one end and its lid on the other end.

If you find a caterpillar whose food you do not know, collect several plants. Put them with the caterpillar in a jar. Look after a few hours to see which it eats.

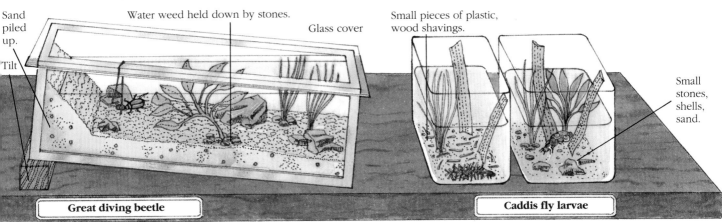

Sand piled up.

Tilt

Water weed held down by stones.

Glass cover

Small pieces of plastic, wood shavings.

Small stones, shells, sand.

Great diving beetle

Caddis fly larvae

Great diving beetles and water boatmen are very fierce, so keep each one on its own. Feed them on maggots or raw meat attached to a thread, and change daily.

See how caddis fly larvae make their protective cases. Collect several caddis flies and carefully remove the larvae from their cases by prodding them with

the blunt end of a pin. Put them in separate aquariums with different materials in each, and watch what happens. Feed them on water weed.

Common insects to spot

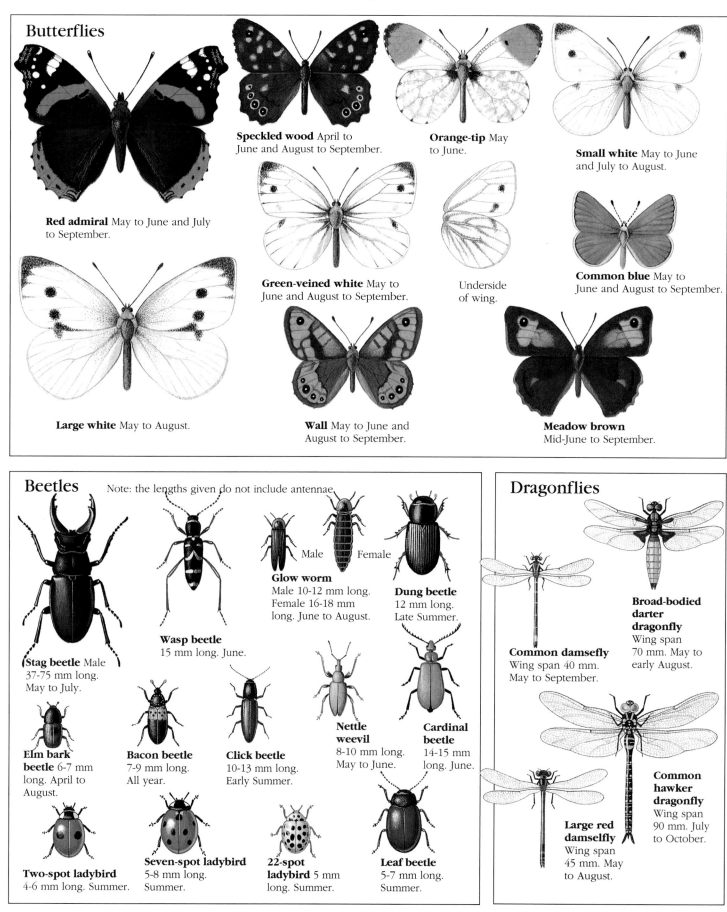

Butterflies

Speckled wood April to June and August to September.

Orange-tip May to June.

Small white May to June and July to August.

Red admiral May to June and July to September.

Green-veined white May to June and August to September.

Underside of wing.

Common blue May to June and August to September.

Large white May to August.

Wall May to June and August to September.

Meadow brown Mid-June to September.

Beetles

Note: the lengths given do not include antennae.

Glow worm
Male 10-12 mm long. Female 16-18 mm long. June to August.

Male   Female

Dung beetle 12 mm long. Late Summer.

Wasp beetle 15 mm long. June.

Stag beetle Male 37-75 mm long. May to July.

Nettle weevil 8-10 mm long. May to June.

Cardinal beetle 14-15 mm long. June.

Elm bark beetle 6-7 mm long. April to August.

Bacon beetle 7-9 mm long. All year.

Click beetle 10-13 mm long. Early Summer.

Two-spot ladybird 4-6 mm long. Summer.

Seven-spot ladybird 5-8 mm long. Summer.

22-spot ladybird 5 mm long. Summer.

Leaf beetle 5-7 mm long. Summer.

Dragonflies

Broad-bodied darter dragonfly Wing span 70 mm. May to early August.

Common damsefly Wing span 40 mm. May to September.

Common hawker dragonfly Wing span 90 mm. July to October.

Large red damselfly Wing span 45 mm. May to August.

28 Each caption tells you the time of year you are most likely to see the insect. The butterflies and moths are drawn life size. The beetles and dragonflies are not.

Moths

Buff-tip July to August.

Eyed hawkmoth May to July.

Scalloped oak July to August.

Yellowtail July to August.

Small magpie May to mid-July.

Angle shades May to October.

Magpie July to mid-August.

Vapourer Late August to October.

Blood-vein May to September.

Silver-Y Migratory (June to October).

Burnished brass June to September.

Puss moth (male) May to June.

Poplar hawkmoth May to August.

Pale tussock May to June.

Brimstone May to June and August to September.

Dot June to August.

Lackey July to August.

Female

Male

Herald Early spring to autumn.

Ghost swift June to July.

Drinker June to mid-August.

Six-spot burnet Late June to mid-August.

Remember, if you cannot see the insect you want to identify on these pages, turn to the page earlier in the book which deals with the kind of place where you found the insect.

More common insects to spot

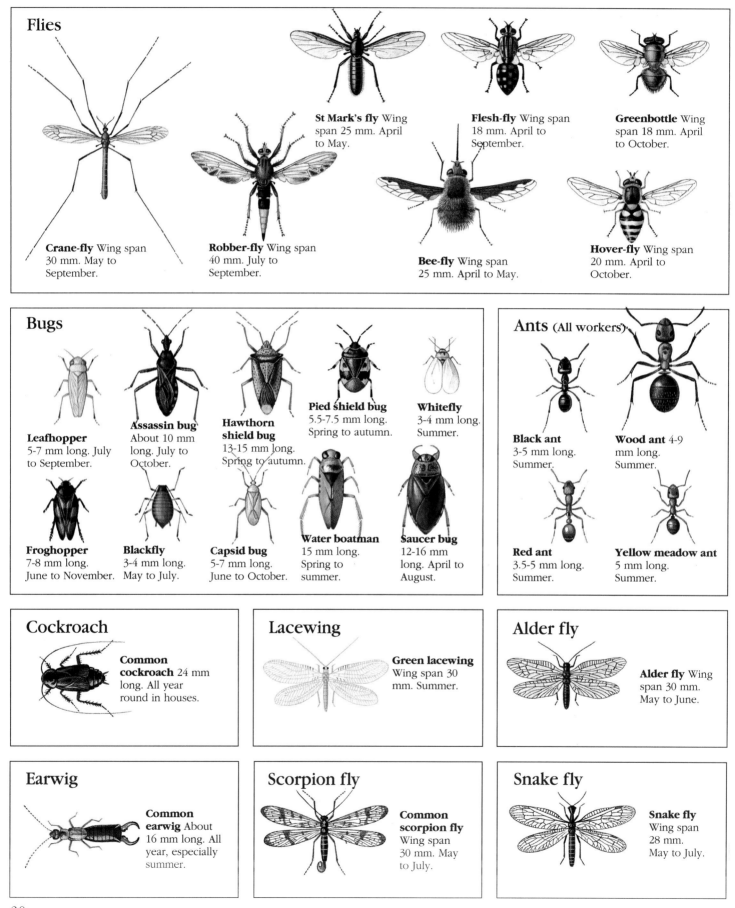

Flies

St Mark's fly Wing span 25 mm. April to May.

Flesh-fly Wing span 18 mm. April to September.

Greenbottle Wing span 18 mm. April to October.

Crane-fly Wing span 30 mm. May to September.

Robber-fly Wing span 40 mm. July to September.

Bee-fly Wing span 25 mm. April to May.

Hover-fly Wing span 20 mm. April to October.

Bugs

Leafhopper 5-7 mm long. July to September.

Assassin bug About 10 mm long. July to October.

Hawthorn shield bug 13-15 mm long. Spring to autumn.

Pied shield bug 5.5-7.5 mm long. Spring to autumn.

Whitefly 3-4 mm long. Summer.

Froghopper 7-8 mm long. June to November.

Blackfly 3-4 mm long. May to July.

Capsid bug 5-7 mm long. June to October.

Water boatman 15 mm long. Spring to summer.

Saucer bug 12-16 mm long. April to August.

Ants (All workers)

Black ant 3-5 mm long. Summer.

Wood ant 4-9 mm long. Summer.

Red ant 3.5-5 mm long. Summer.

Yellow meadow ant 5 mm long. Summer.

Cockroach

Common cockroach 24 mm long. All year round in houses.

Lacewing

Green lacewing Wing span 30 mm. Summer.

Alder fly

Alder fly Wing span 30 mm. May to June.

Earwig

Common earwig About 16 mm long. All year, especially summer.

Scorpion fly

Common scorpion fly Wing span 30 mm. May to July.

Snake fly

Snake fly Wing span 28 mm. May to July.

Each caption tells you the time of year you are most likely to see the insect. The lengths given do not include antennae.

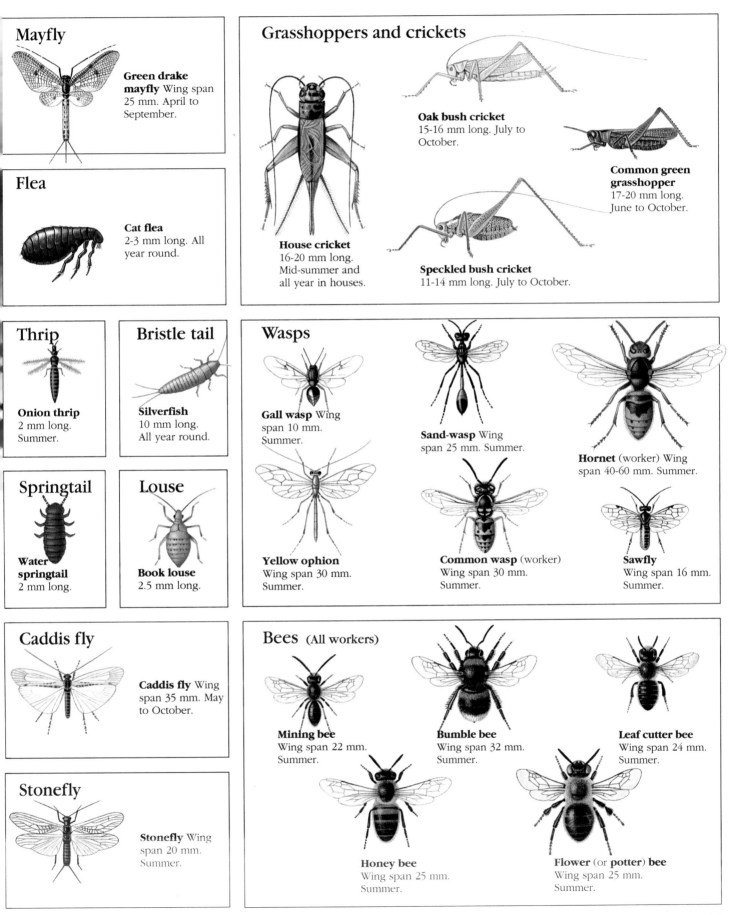

Mayfly

Green drake mayfly Wing span 25 mm. April to September.

Flea

Cat flea 2-3 mm long. All year round.

Grasshoppers and crickets

Oak bush cricket 15-16 mm long. July to October.

Common green grasshopper 17-20 mm long. June to October.

House cricket 16-20 mm long. Mid-summer and all year in houses.

Speckled bush cricket 11-14 mm long. July to October.

Thrip

Onion thrip 2 mm long. Summer.

Bristle tail

Silverfish 10 mm long. All year round.

Springtail

Water springtail 2 mm long.

Louse

Book louse 2.5 mm long.

Wasps

Gall wasp Wing span 10 mm. Summer.

Sand-wasp Wing span 25 mm. Summer.

Hornet (worker) Wing span 40-60 mm. Summer.

Yellow ophion Wing span 30 mm. Summer.

Common wasp (worker) Wing span 30 mm. Summer.

Sawfly Wing span 16 mm. Summer.

Caddis fly

Caddis fly Wing span 35 mm. May to October.

Stonefly

Stonefly Wing span 20 mm. Summer.

Bees (All workers)

Mining bee Wing span 22 mm. Summer.

Bumble bee Wing span 32 mm. Summer.

Leaf cutter bee Wing span 24 mm. Summer.

Honey bee Wing span 25 mm. Summer.

Flower (or **potter**) **bee** Wing span 25 mm. Summer.

Remember, if you cannot see the insect you want to identify on these pages, turn to the page earlier in the book which deals with the kind of place where you found the insect.

Index

Books

The Insects in your Garden. Harold Oldroyd (Kestrel)
Bees. Young Naturalist Book (Priory Press)
Wasps. Young Naturalist Book (Priory Press)
Insects. Collins' Green Guide (Collins)
Observer's Insects. (Penguin)

Clubs and societies

The Amateur Entomologists' Society (355 Hounslow Road, Hanworth, Feltham, Middlesex TW13 5DP) has younger members as well as adults, who can exchange letters and news through the society.
The Council for Environmental Conservation (Zoological Gardens, Regents Park, London NW1 4RY) will supply the addresses of your local

Natural History Societies. Send a stamped, addressed envelope for a list.
The Royal Society for Nature Conservation (22, The Green, Nettleham, Lincoln LN2 2NR) will give you the address of your **County Naturalist Trust**, which may have a junior branch. Many of the trusts have meetings, lectures, and opportunities for work on reserves.